Cambridge English

Movers

AUTHENTIC EXAMINATION PAPERS

1

T0363846

STUDENT'S BOOK

Cambridge University Press
www.cambridge.org/elt

Cambridge Assessment English
www.cambridgeenglish.org

Information on this title: www.cambridge.org/9781316635902

© Cambridge University Press and UCLES 2017

First published 2017

40 39 38 37 36 35 34 33 32 31 30 29 28 27 26 25 24 23 22 21

Printed in Dubai by Oriental Press

A catalogue record for this publication is available from the British Library

ISBN 978-1-316-63590-2 Student's Book
ISBN 978-1-316-63594-0 Answer Booklet
ISBN 978-1-316-63598-8 Audio CDs (2)

The publishers have no responsibility for the persistence or accuracy of URLs
for external or third-party internet websites referred to in this publication, and
do not guarantee that any content on such websites is, or will remain, accurate
or appropriate. Information regarding prices, travel timetables, and other factual
information given in this work is correct at the time of first printing but the
publishers do not guarantee the accuracy of such information thereafter.

Cover Illustration: (T) Happy_Inside/iStock/Getty Images Plus; (B) adekvat/iStock/Getty Images Plus

Contents

Part 1
– 5 questions –

Listen and draw lines. There is one example.

Daisy   Sally   David   Jane

Jim   Fred   Peter

Part 2

– 5 questions –

Listen and write. There is one example.

Sports centre

	Boy's age:	.... II ....
1	Favourite sport:	....
2	Lives in:	.... Street
3	Comes to sports centre by:	....
4	Comes to sports centre after:	....
5	Often buys some:	....

Part 3

– 5 questions –

Sally is telling Mr Castle about the people in her family and their jobs. What work do these people do?

Listen and write a letter in each box. There is one example.

her dad   A

her mum   ☐

her sister   ☐

her uncle   ☐

her aunt   ☐

her grandpa   ☐

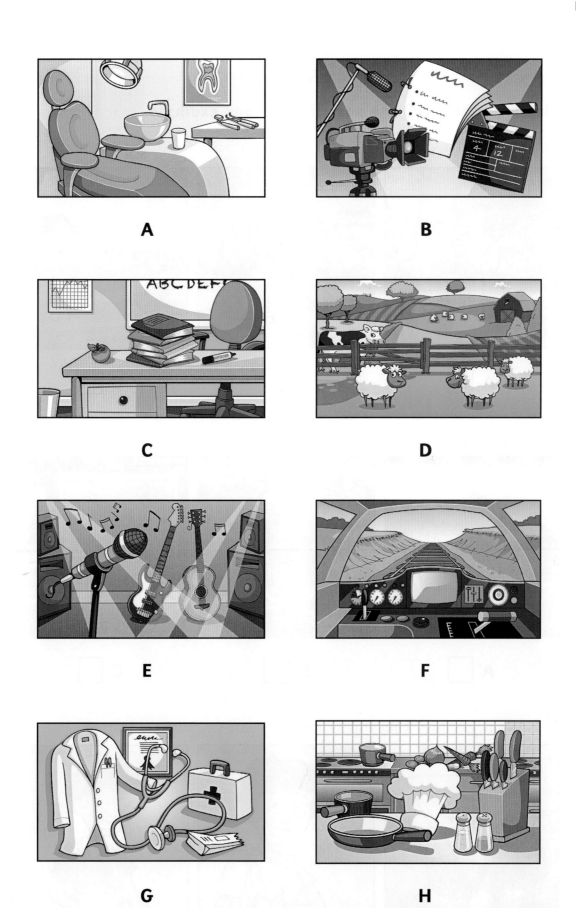

A

B

C

D

E

F

G

H

Part 4
– 5 questions –

Listen and tick (✔) the box. There is one example.

Where is Charlie's house?

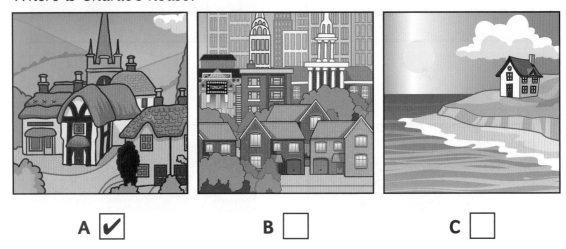

A ✔   B ☐   C ☐

1   What did Anna do yesterday?

A ☐   B ☐   C ☐

2   What job does Tom's sister have?

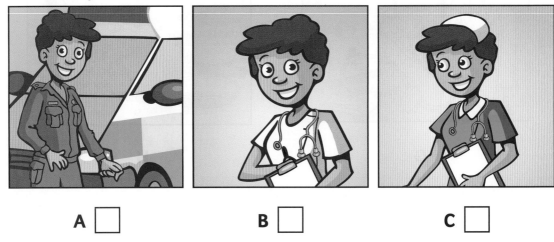

A ☐   B ☐   C ☐

3   What did Alex do on holiday?

A ☐   B ☐   C ☐

4   How did Jill help her mum and dad?

A ☐   B ☐   C ☐

5   Which toy did Jack buy for his sister?

A ☐   B ☐   C ☐

Part 5

– 5 questions –

Listen and colour and write. There is one example.

Blank Page

Reading and Writing

Part 1

– 5 questions –

Look and read. Choose the correct words and write them on the lines. There is one example.

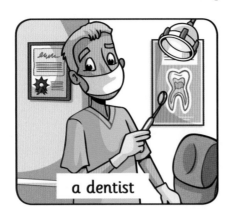

a dentist

a milkshake

coffee

a nurse

a farmer

a shower

a lamp

a salad

Example

This person helps people who aren't
well in hospital.

.... *a nurse* ....

Questions

1 This has lots of green vegetables in it,
but you don't cook it.

....

2 You stand under this when you want
to wash.

....

3 This person works outside in the fields.

....

4 Some people put milk in this brown drink.

....

5 This person helps people when their
teeth hurt.

....

Part 2

– 6 questions –

Read the text and choose the best answer.

Fred and Vicky are talking about their pets.

Example

Fred:	Our new kitten is so funny!

Vicky:	A Do they laugh?
	B Is it?
	C Are those new?

Questions

1 **Vicky:**	Why is your kitten funny?

Fred:	A You all smiled.
	B It loves hiding.
	C I can't tell them.

2   **Vicky:**   Does your kitten like playing games?

      Fred: A   Yes, that's right.

                                   B   No, I can't today.

                                   C   OK, let's do that.

3   **Vicky:**   What's your kitten's favourite toy?

      Fred: A   By that red blanket.

                                     B   It's another one.

                                   C   A big, round ball.

4   **Fred:**   How old is your puppy now, Vicky?

      Vicky: A   It's the biggest one.

                                     B   Twelve weeks.

                                   C   It's great, thanks.

5   **Fred:**   Does your puppy sleep outside?

      Vicky: A   Yes, we can do that.

                                     B   Its bed is very small.

                                   C   No, it's too young.

6   **Fred:**   I'd like to have another pet.

      Vicky: A   Me too!

                                   B   How often?

                                   C   Well done!

Part 3

– 6 questions –

Read the story. Choose a word from the box. Write the correct word next to numbers 1–5. There is one example.

Zoe is the youngest of the three .... *girls* .... in her family.

Sometimes her two older sisters called her 'baby Zoe'. 'I'm not a baby,'

Zoe said. 'I'm ten now!'

Last Sunday Zoe's family had a great day. They

(1) .... to the forest, went for a very

(2) .... walk and had a picnic. Then Zoe's dad

read his book, her mother went to sleep and her sisters sat and talked.

Zoe climbed to the top of a tall tree. From the top of the tree, Zoe could

see lots of big, black **(3)** .... above the mountains.

'Oh no!' she thought. 'Rain!' She climbed down the tree and ran to tell her

family. 'Quickly! Come on! Back to the car!'

When they all jumped up and started to put the

(4) .... and bowls back in the picnic bag, Zoe

smiled. 'I'm not a baby. I'm talking like a grown-up and they're all

(5) .... to me!' she thought.

Example

girls

listening

clouds

strong

drove

glasses

shouted

crying

long

(6) Now choose the best name for the story.

Tick one box.

The baby's favourite tree ☐

What a windy day! ☐

Zoe helps her family ☐

Part 4
– 5 questions –

Read the text. Choose the right words and write them on the lines.

Bats

Example | Bats are small animals that can fly. ....There............... are

many different kinds of bat and they live in many parts of the world.

1 | Some live in jungles, some live in trees ....

2 | inside houses, but you don't often see ....

Most bats sleep in the day and only fly at night. Bats can't see very

3 | well with .... eyes, but they are all very

4 | good .... flying. They can fly very quickly.

Small bats sometimes eat mice, but bigger bats often eat fruit and

5 | drink juice that they .... in flowers.

Example	There	Most	Here
1	because	or	when
2	it	him	them
3	its	their	our
4	to	at	in
5	find	finds	finding

Part 5

– 7 questions –

Look at the pictures and read the story. Write some words to complete the sentences about the story. You can use 1, 2 or 3 words.

<u>Fishing in the lake</u>

Sally and her brother, Peter, live next to a lake and they love swimming and fishing in it. They often fish from the end of their garden, but last Saturday, they went fishing in another part of the lake. But there were no fish there.

'This is boring,' Sally said. She put her fishing things down and took off her shoes. Then she put her feet in the water because it was a hot and sunny day.

Examples

Sally and Peter enjoy ..<u>swimming and fishing</u>.. in the lake near their house.

The children fished in another part of the lake last ....<u>Saturday</u>........... .

Questions

1   Sally stopped fishing because there were .... in the water that day.

2   Because it was hot and sunny, Sally .... in the lake.

'Sally, look!' Peter said. 'I think I can see a lake monster!' Sally jumped up to look, but when she did that, she dropped her shoes in the water!

Then she got angry with Peter because there was no monster. 'Now I haven't got my shoes!' she said. 'It's not funny!'

Peter looked down in the water. He could see Sally's orange shoes at the bottom of the lake.

3   Peter said he saw a ....

4   When she jumped up, Sally .... in the lake.

5   Sally was angry because her shoes were at .... of the lake.

'Well, let's try to catch your shoes now!' Peter said. He fished them out of the lake.

Sally was happy again.

When they got home, their mum was in the kitchen.

'Did you catch any fish?' she asked.

She laughed when Peter said, 'Yes we caught two Orange Shoe Fish!'

6   Sally .... when Peter caught her shoes.

7   When the children told her about the two orange shoe fish, their mum ....

Blank Page

Part 6
– 6 questions –

Look and read and write.

Examples

Where is the tree with purple leaves? ....On the island..............

The ....monkey............ is holding some watermelon.

Questions

Complete the sentences.

1   The pink .... is smaller than the white one.

2   There are two coconuts in ....

Answer the questions.

3   What is the weather like?   ....

4   What is the oldest pirate pointing at?   ....

Now write two sentences about the picture.

5   ....

6   ....

Listening

Part 1
– 5 questions –

Listen and draw lines. There is one example.

Lily   Daisy   Julia   Jim

Sally   Mary   Nick

Part 2

– 5 questions –

Listen and write. There is one example.

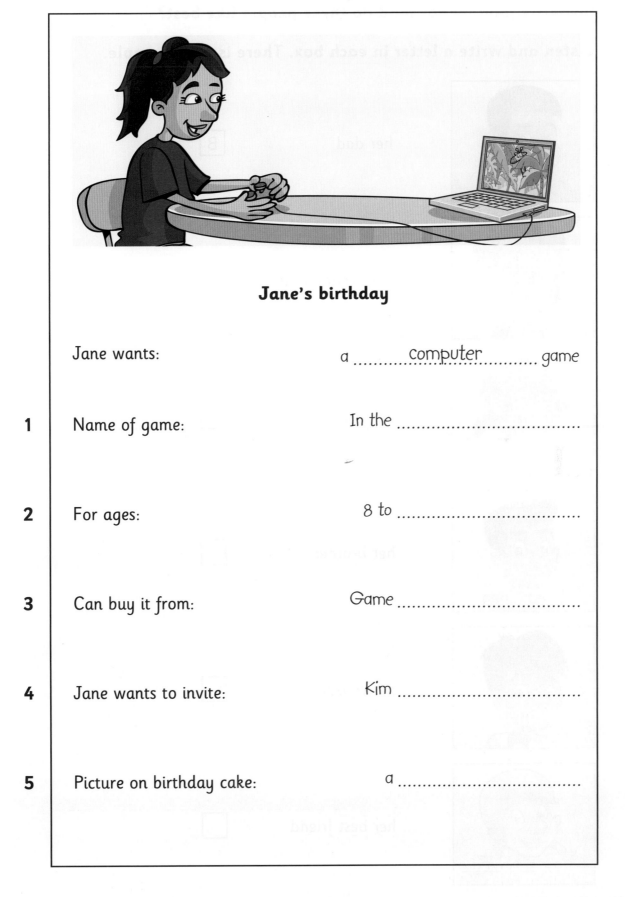

Jane's birthday

Jane wants: a .... computer .... game

1 Name of game: In the ....

2 For ages: 8 to ....

3 Can buy it from: Game ....

4 Jane wants to invite: Kim ....

5 Picture on birthday cake: a ....

Part 3

– 5 questions –

Zoe is telling her grandfather about people she knows and their favourite food. What food do these people like best?

Listen and write a letter in each box. There is one example.

her dad   [B]

her grandmother   [ ]

her sister   [ ]

her brother   [ ]

her cousin   [ ]

her best friend   [ ]

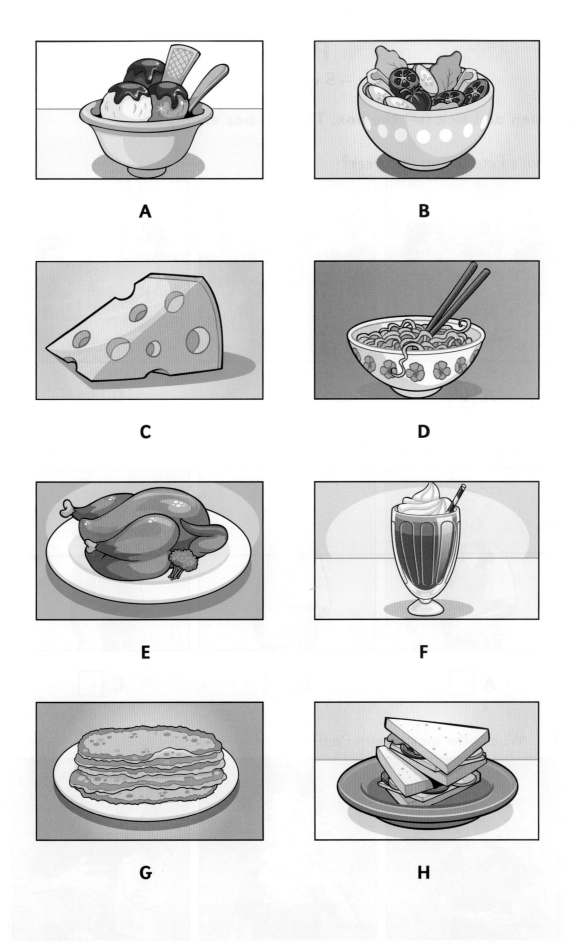

A

B

C

D

E

F

G

H

Part 4

– 5 questions –

Listen and tick (✔) the box. There is one example.

What's Peter doing this week?

A ✔   B ☐   C ☐

1 Which man is Sam's piano teacher?

A ☐   B ☐   C ☐

2 What's the matter with Paul?

A ☐   B ☐   C ☐

3 Where's Pat?

A ☐   B ☐   C ☐

4 Where did Alex go yesterday?

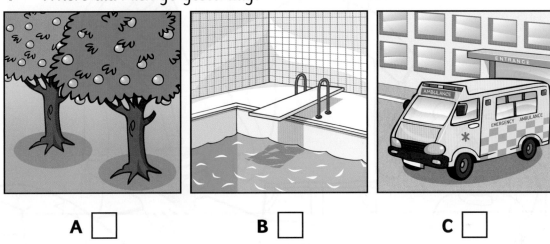

A ☐   B ☐   C ☐

5 How did May come to school today?

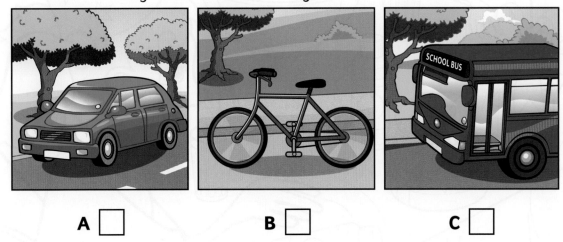

A ☐   B ☐   C ☐

Part 5

– 5 questions –

Listen and colour and write. There is one example.

Blank Page

Reading and Writing

Part 1
– 5 questions –

Look and read. Choose the correct words and write them on the lines. There is one example.

a picnic

a circus

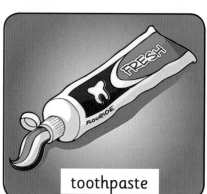

toothpaste

coffee

a market

a shower

cheese

a field

Example

You sit and eat this outside. .... a picnic ....

Questions

1   You stand and wash your body under this.

....

2   Farmers sometimes make this food from cow's or goat's milk.

....

3   People go there to have fun and you can see clowns.

....

4   Some animals like sheep live in this.

....

5   You need this in the bathroom in the morning and at night.

....

Part 2
– 6 questions –

Read the text and choose the best answer.

Example

Peter:	Here are my holiday photos, Vicky!
Vicky:	(A) Wow, they're great!
	B Hello, I'm Vicky.
	C Oh, they aren't here!

Questions

1 Peter: I like going on holiday.

      Vicky:

         A   So do I.
         B   I am too.
         C   Go there now.

2 **Peter:** Where do you and your family go, Vicky?

Vicky:
A When it's sunny.
B By train.
C To the beach.

3 **Peter:** What do you do on holiday?

Vicky:
A You do it often.
B We do lots of different things.
C I do it very carefully.

4 **Vicky:** I love sailing most. What's your favourite hobby, Peter?

Peter:
A I don't know.
B I think he's nice.
C What a good idea!

5 **Vicky:** Well, do you like going to famous places?

Peter:
A It's wrong!
B Sometimes!
C Give it to me please!

6 **Vicky:** My dad likes fishing when we're on holiday.

Peter:
A Yes, let's go. Look at this photo!
B He's well. Look at this photo!
C Mine likes sitting in the sun. Look at this photo!

Part 3

– 6 questions –

Read the story. Choose a word from the box. Write the correct word next to numbers 1–5. There is one example.

Doctor Brown had a nice new car and he ....*loved*............

driving it to the hospital every morning. Last Tuesday, the

(1) .... was terrible and when Doctor Brown

drove down Top Road, he saw four people at the bus stop. They didn't

look happy in the wind and the rain. One of them was Paul Parks.

Doctor Brown knew Paul. He stopped his car and said, 'Don't

(2) .... for the bus this morning, Paul. I can take

you to work.'

'Thank you! Can you take Jim too?' Paul asked. 'He works with me at the

(3) ....'

'And can you take my two friends, too?' Jim asked. 'They work at the

library.'

Doctor Brown **(4)** .... and said, 'Yes, OK! Get in the

car all of you.'

Doctor Brown started the car again. 'This morning, I'm not a doctor. I'm a

bus **(5)** .... !'

Example

loved

tickets

supermarket

driver

ride

snowed

weather

laughed

wait

(6) **Now choose the best name for the story.**

Tick one box.

Doctor Brown's new nurse ☐

Doctor Brown's best breakfast ☐

Doctor Brown's busy morning ☐

Part 4

– 5 questions –

Read the text. Choose the right words and write them on the lines.

Dolphins

Dolphins are like small whales and some of them have

Example ....more................... than 100 teeth! Dolphins don't need to

1   drink because .... is lots of water in the fish

that they eat.

2   Dolphins sometimes play .... people in the

water and they swim in front of boats too.

3   Dolphins .... in the sea in families and the

4   parents teach .... babies to catch fish. They learn

very quickly!

5   Dolphins can't say words, ... they can 'sing' and

'talk'. They're very clever!

Example	many	more	most
1	where	here	there
2	to	with	from
3	lived	living	live
4	they	them	their
5	but	and	or

Part 5
– 7 questions –

Look at the pictures and read the story. Write some words to complete the sentences about the story. You can use 1, 2 or 3 words.

<u>Cloudy and the lost scarf</u>

Julia's home was in the countryside. One day Julia and her black and grey dog, Cloudy, went for a long walk in the forest. They saw a white rabbit. It hopped behind some tall grass, and Cloudy quickly ran to try to catch it.

'Naughty dog! Come back here!' shouted Julia. Cloudy came back but there was something white in its mouth. 'Oh no!' Julia thought.

Examples

Julia had a ....*black and grey*........ dog, which was called Cloudy.

When Julia and Cloudy walked in the forest they saw a white
..............*rabbit*.............. .

Questions

1   Cloudy tried .... the rabbit.

But it wasn't the rabbit. It was a beautiful white scarf! Cloudy dropped it on the ground and Julia picked it up. 'This scarf looks new. I must try to find the person who lost it,' she thought.

Julia put the scarf round her neck and walked slowly back home. 'Cloudy!' she called, 'Come on! Good dog!'

2 There was a .... in Cloudy's mouth.

3 Julia wanted to find the .... the scarf.

4 Julia went home with the white scarf round ....

Julia opened the door and saw her Aunt Daisy and Mum in the hall.

'Hello Aunt Daisy!' she said and took off her coat. 'Look, Mum. Cloudy found this scarf on our walk.'

Aunt Daisy looked very surprised. 'That's my scarf,' she said. 'I bought it yesterday morning, then I lost it in the afternoon when I went for a walk.'

Julia gave her aunt the scarf.

'Thank you!' Aunt Daisy said. 'And thank you too, Cloudy!'

5 Julia's .... was in the hall with Mum when Julia went home.

6 Aunt Daisy was .... when she saw the white scarf.

7 Aunt Daisy said 'thank you' to Julia and to ....

Blank Page

Part 6
– 6 questions –

Look and read and write.

Examples

There is only one white ......cloud in the sky...... .

Where is the bear jumping? ......into the river...... .

Questions

Complete the sentences.

1   The green .... is sitting on the rock.

2   There is a fish at the bottom of ....

Answer the questions.

3   Where is the snow?   ....

4   Who is the boy smiling at?   ....

Now write two sentences about the picture.

5   ....

6   ....

Listening

Part 1
– 5 questions –

Listen and draw lines. There is one example.

Fred   Vicky   Jim   Mary

Paul   Daisy   Jack

Part 2

– 5 questions –

Listen and write. There is one example.

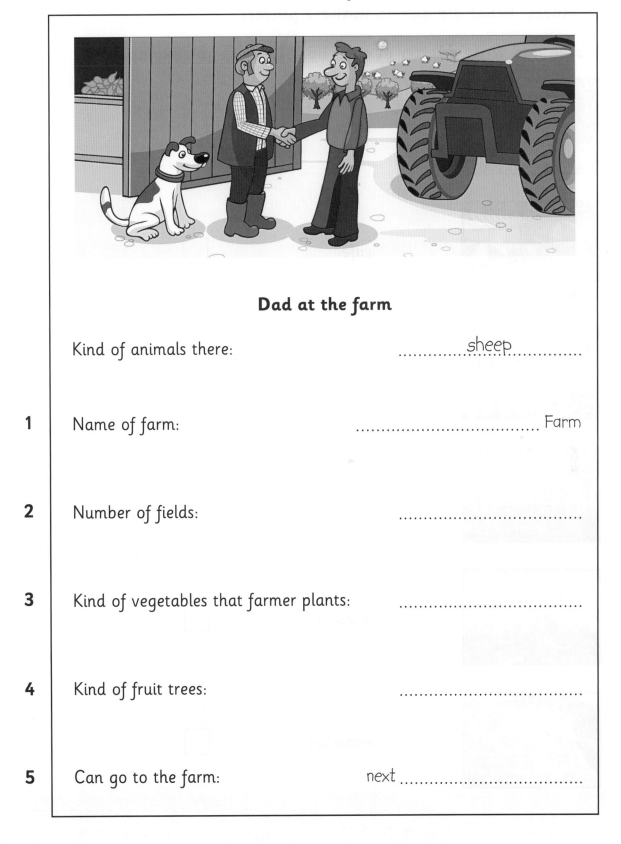

Dad at the farm

Kind of animals there: ....sheep................

1 Name of farm: .... Farm

2 Number of fields: ....

3 Kind of vegetables that farmer plants: ....

4 Kind of fruit trees: ....

5 Can go to the farm: next ....

Part 3

– 5 questions –

Zoe slept at her grandparents' house all week. They went to lots of places. What did Zoe do in these places?

Listen and write a letter in each box. There is one example.

	village	C
	café	☐
	lake	☐
	cinema	☐
	mountain	☐
	waterfall	☐

A

B

C

D

E

F

G

H

Part 4

– 5 questions –

Listen and tick (✔) the box. There is one example.

What does Jane want to put on?

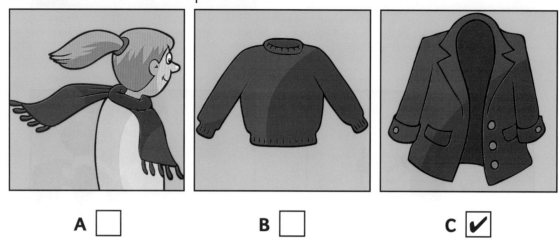

A ☐   B ☐   C ✔

1   Where's Jim now?

A ☐   B ☐   C ☐

2   What's Peter's favourite sport?

A ☐   B ☐   C ☐

3 What can Lucy have to drink?

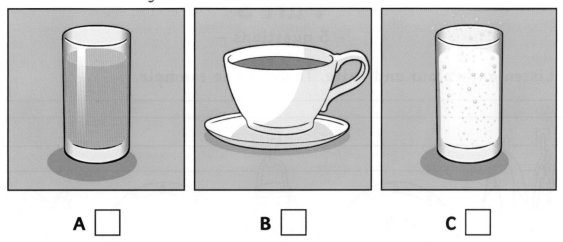

A ☐   B ☐   C ☐

4 Where are Uncle Nick's roller skates?

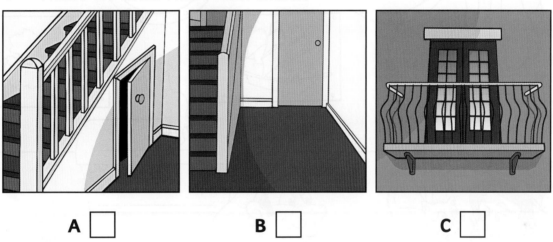

A ☐   B ☐   C ☐

5 Which girl is Sue?

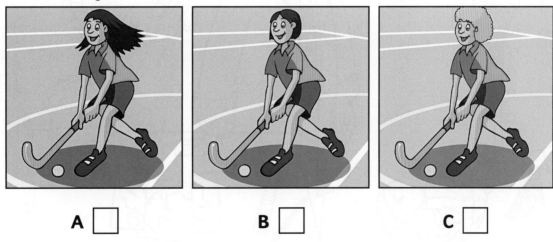

A ☐   B ☐   C ☐

Part 5
– 5 questions –

Listen and colour and write. There is one example.

Blank Page

Reading and Writing

Part 1

– 5 questions –

Look and read. Choose the correct words and write them on the lines. There is one example.

a zoo

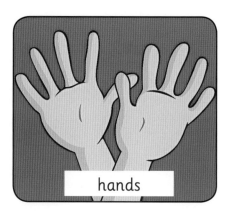

hands

a supermarket

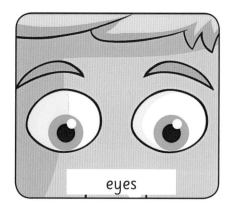

eyes

a playground

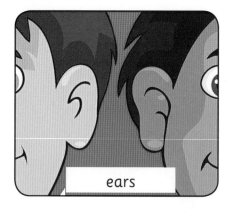

ears

a city

a funfair

Example

Children run, shout and play games in this place which is outside.

.............a playground.........

Questions

1 You can hold and pick up things with these parts of your body.

....

2 Animals like pandas, penguins and kangaroos sometimes live here.

....

3 You can buy vegetables and other kinds of food from this shop.

....

4 These are part of your body and you listen with them.

....

5 There are lots of cars, buildings and people in this place.

....

Part 2
– 6 questions –

Read the text and choose the best answer.

Example

Jim:	My grandma bought me a car yesterday!

Paul:	(A) Wow!
	B It's good.
	C He's fantastic!

Questions

1 Jim:	It's a toy car like the one in my favourite film. I love cars.

Paul:	A Come on.
	B Me too.
	C See you.

2 Jim: Have you got lots of cars?

    Paul:
- A Yes, there are.
- B Yes, twenty.
- C Yes, I know.

3 Jim: How often do you watch films?

    Paul:
- A At weekends.
- B I watched last Wednesday.
- C You do it every day.

4 Jim: What kind of films do you like?

    Paul:
- A I'd like them.
- B That's my favourite.
- C All films.

5 Jim: I like going to the cinema, but I think watching DVDs at home is better.

    Paul:
- A What a great film.
- B So do I.
- C Here you are.

6 Jim: How about coming to my house on Saturday to watch a DVD?

    Paul:
- A Well done!
- B That's it!
- C Good idea!

Part 3

– 6 questions –

Read the story. Choose a word from the box. Write the correct word next to numbers 1–5. There is one example.

Vicky and her younger sister, Daisy, were in their ....*bedroom*............ .

'Will you play a game with me? I want to be a doctor,' asked Daisy. Daisy

was **(1)** .... when Vicky said 'Yes'. Most days, Vicky

said 'No'.

Daisy got her toys out of the **(2)** .... by her bed. She

asked them, 'What's the matter?'

She looked into her crocodile's mouth. 'I think you have

(3) .... ,' she said.

Vicky said, 'He must go to bed.' And Daisy put the crocodile in her bed.

Then Daisy looked at her robot. 'You are too **(4)** ....

You have a temperature,' she said.

'Bed!' said Vicky, and Daisy put the robot in the bed.

'This doll is thirsty,' said Daisy.

'**(5)** .... more, and go to bed,' Vicky said. Daisy put

the doll in her bed. Then Daisy said, 'Thank you for playing with me, Vicky.

I think you are a good sister, but you aren't a very good doctor. You only

told my toys to go to bed!'

Example

bedroom	comic	hit
toothache	cupboard	hot
strong	surprised	drink

(6)   Now choose the best name for the story.

Tick one box.

Daisy is not well ☐

Vicky sees a nurse ☐

The sisters' game ☐

Part 4

– 5 questions –

Read the text. Choose the right words and write them on the lines.

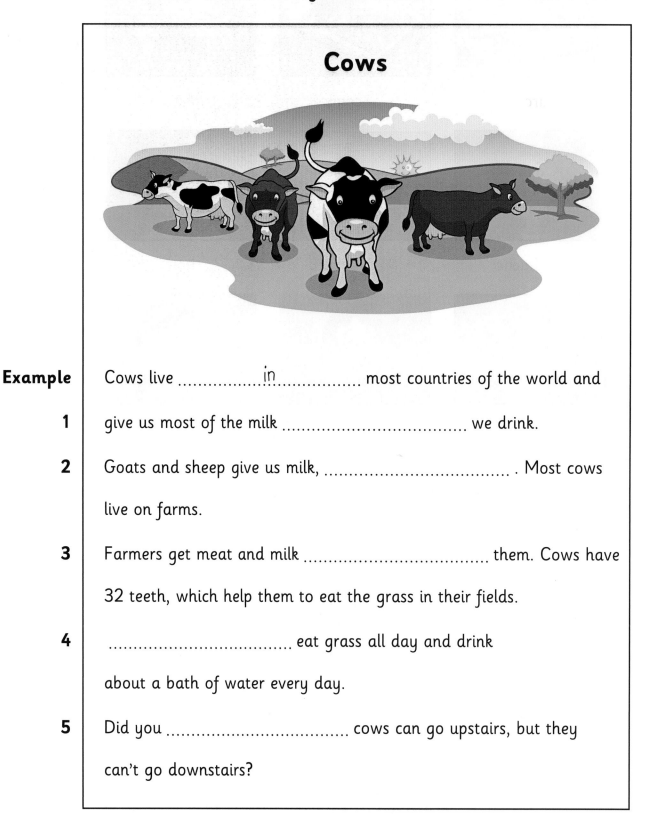

Cows

Example   Cows live ....in.................... most countries of the world and

1   give us most of the milk .... we drink.

2   Goats and sheep give us milk, ... Most cows

live on farms.

3   Farmers get meat and milk .... them. Cows have

32 teeth, which help them to eat the grass in their fields.

4   .... eat grass all day and drink

about a bath of water every day.

5   Did you .... cows can go upstairs, but they

can't go downstairs?

Example	in	at	by
1	that	what	who
2	very	only	too
3	from	of	round
4	We	They	It
5	know	knowing	knew

Part 5
– 7 questions –

Look at the pictures and read the story. Write some words to complete the sentences about the story. You can use 1, 2 or 3 words.

Paul's holiday

Paul lives with his family in Yellow Rock town. He and his sister Sally go to Yellow Rock School.

On the last day of school, Paul's teacher said, 'Listen children, you have homework.' First the children were sad because they had homework, but they were happier when they listened more:

'Your homework is to take a funny holiday photo.'

Examples

Paul lives in ......Yellow Rock town...... with his family.

Sally is the name of Paul's ....sister............. .

Questions

1   At the end of school, Paul's teacher gave the children some
    .... to do.

2   The children's holiday picture had to be ....

Paul went with his family on a beach holiday. They wanted to go to a beach in a sunny country because they lived in a cold, cloudy town.

At their holiday house, Paul and Sally quickly put their bags in their rooms, and ran down to the beach. Then, Paul's mum brought a small picnic and a blanket in a beach bag with her to the beach.

3   Paul and .... went on holiday to a sunny country.

4   Paul's mum took a .... with a picnic and a blanket to the beach.

At the beach Paul's mum smiled. 'I love the sun,' she said. Then big grey clouds hid the sun. It started to rain.

Sally had an idea. She got the blanket and held it above her head. Her mum and dad sat under it too.

'Do you have your phone, Dad?' asked Paul. 'Can I take a photo with it?' Paul's dad gave him his phone and Paul took a photo of them under the blanket.

'Brilliant! That's my homework photo!' he laughed. 'You look very funny!'

5 The sun went behind some .... and it started to rain.

6 Sally sat .... with her mum and dad.

7 Paul asked for his dad's .... to take a photo.

Blank Page

Part 6
– 6 questions –

Look and read and write.

Examples

The teacher has brown hair and a .... *beard* ....

Where is the snail? .... *on the bag* ....

Questions

Complete the sentences.

1   The two .... under the coats are very wet.

2   The boy with blonde hair is looking at   ....

Answer the questions.

3   Where is the clock?   ....

4   What is the teacher pointing at?   ....

Now write two sentences about the picture.

5   ....

6   ....

Find the differences

Picture Story

Fred's always dirty

Fred

Odd-one-out

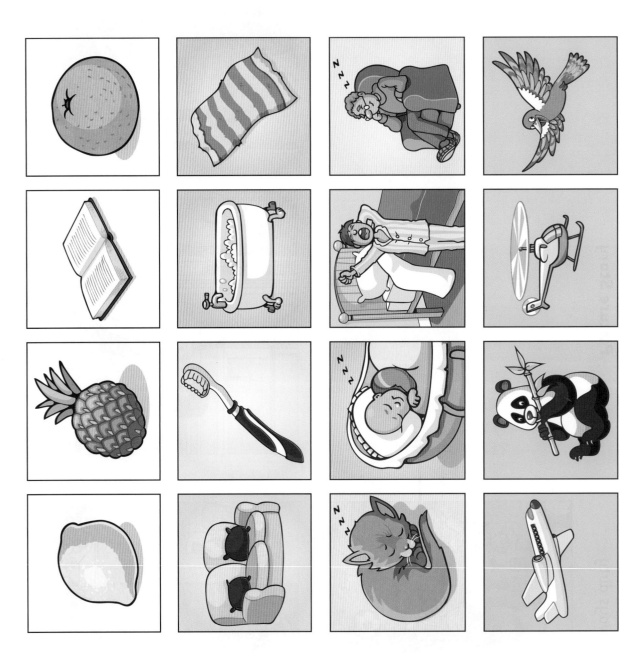

Blank Page

Find the differences

Picture Story

Jane finds the cow

Jane

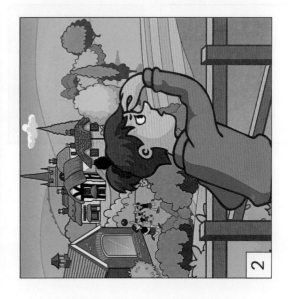

Odd-one-out

Blank Page

Find the differences

Picture Story

Lily loses her mouse

Lily

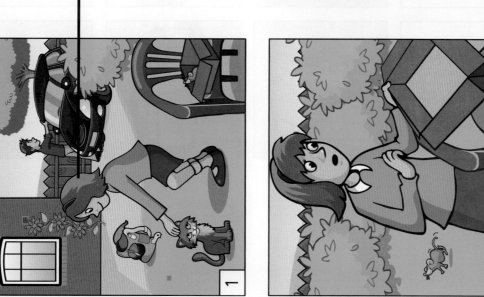

Odd-one-out

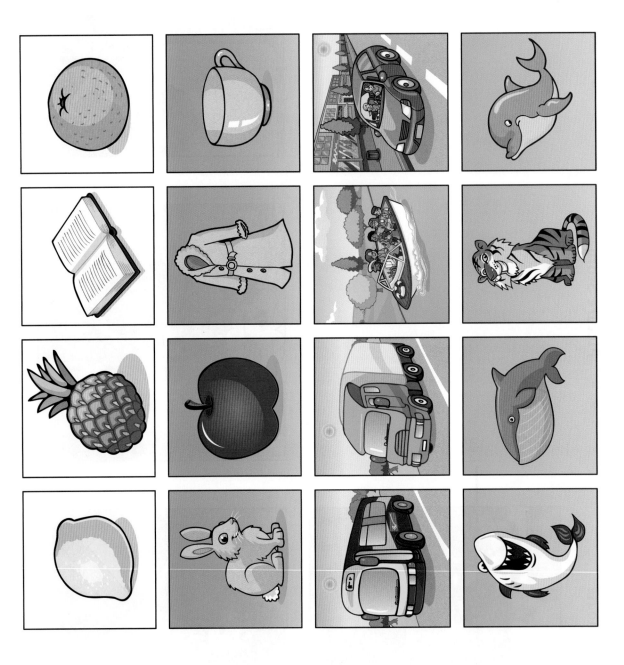